40 Outfits To Style

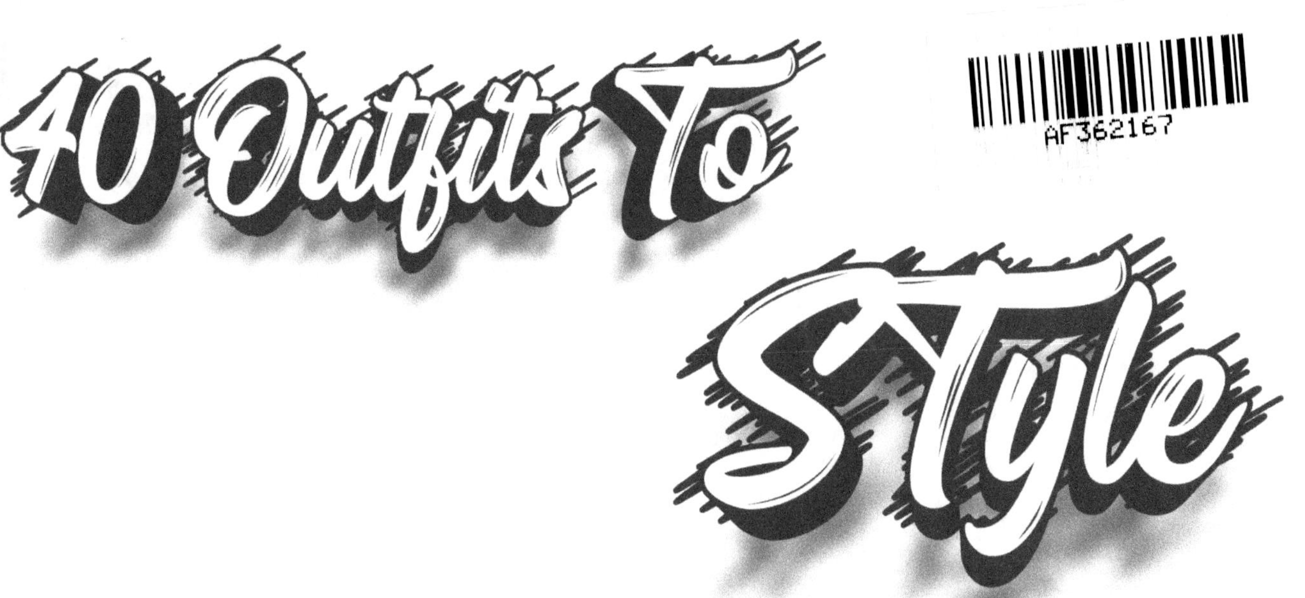

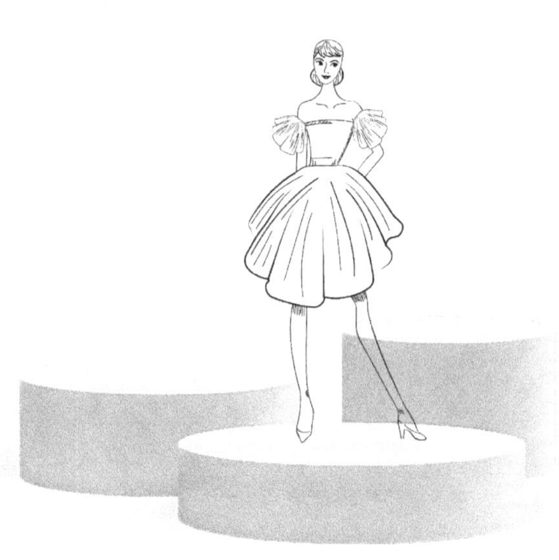

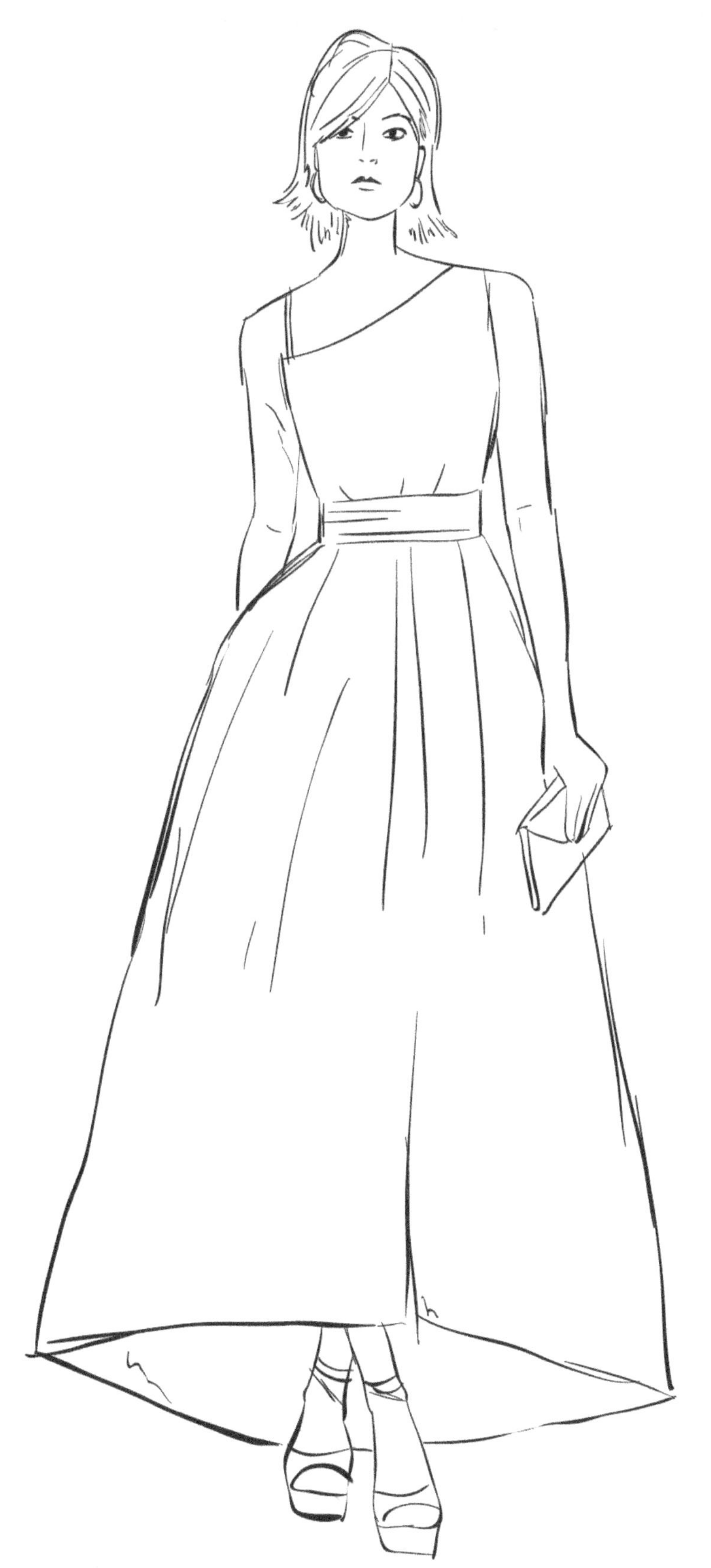

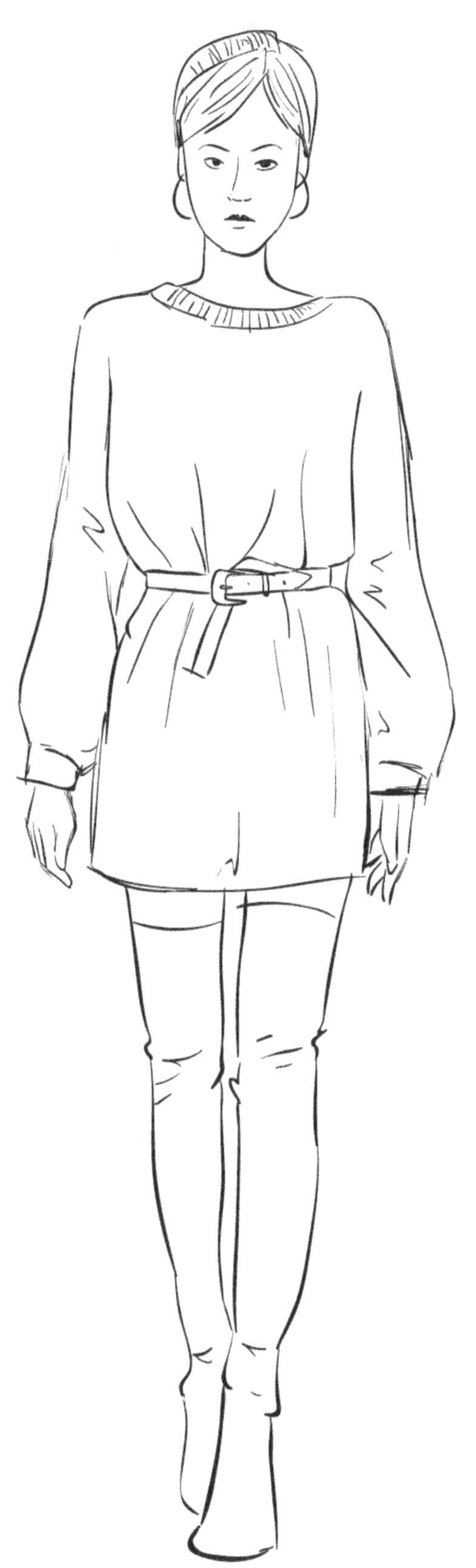

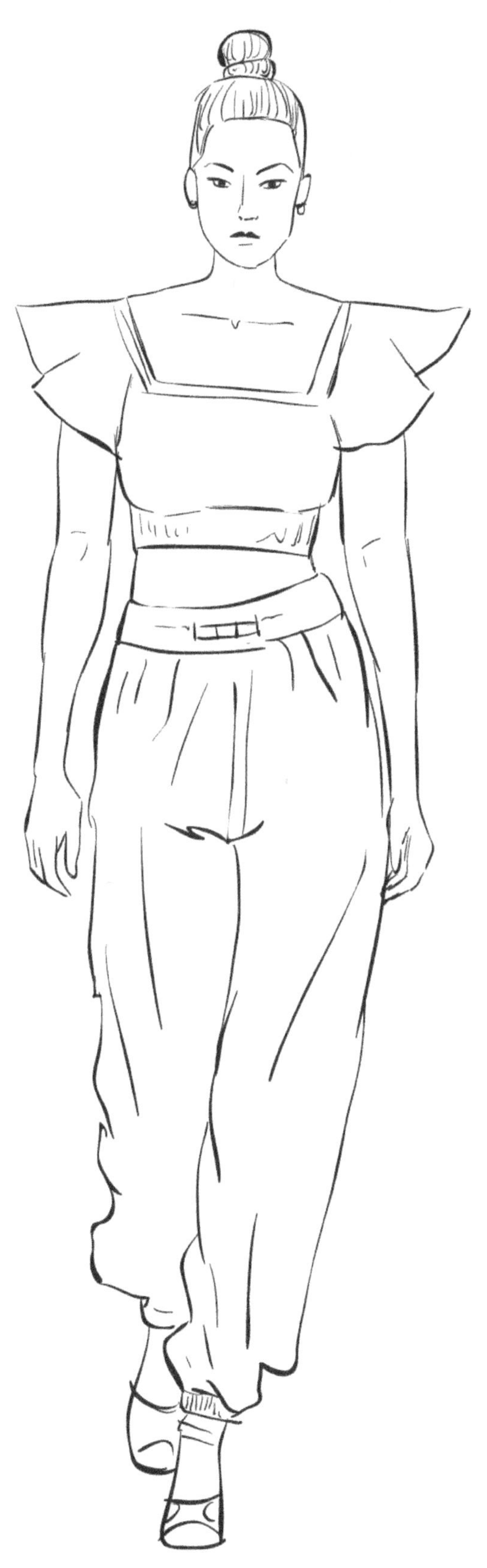

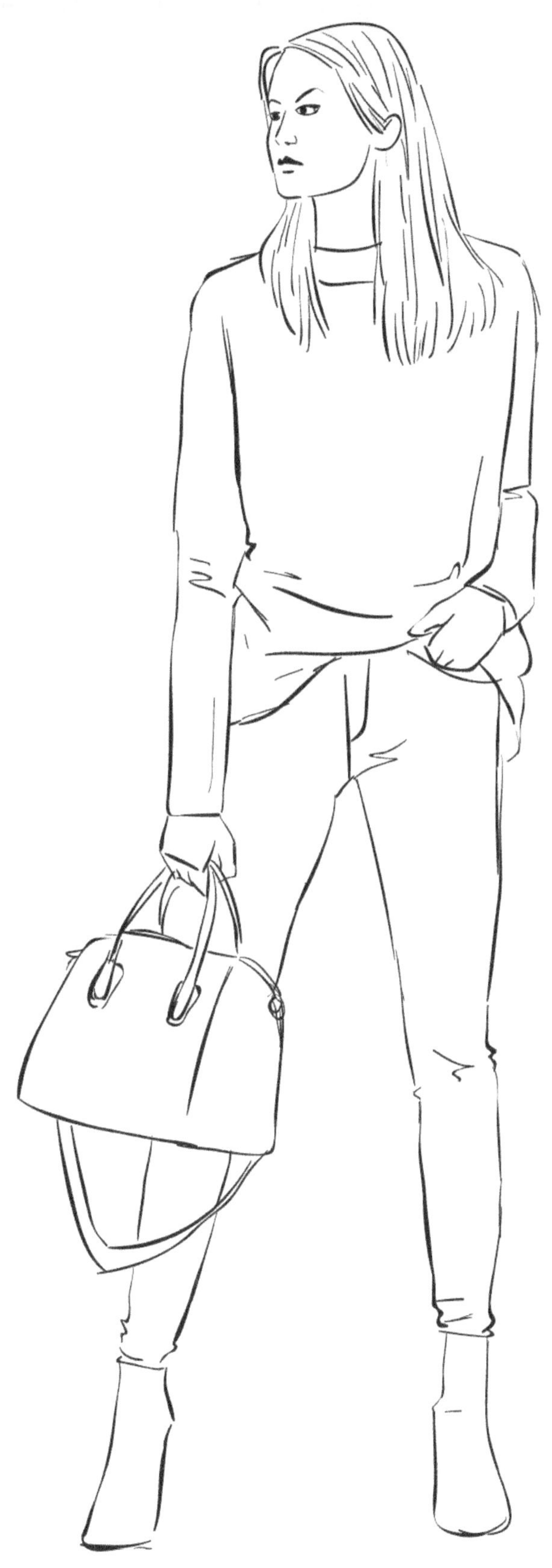

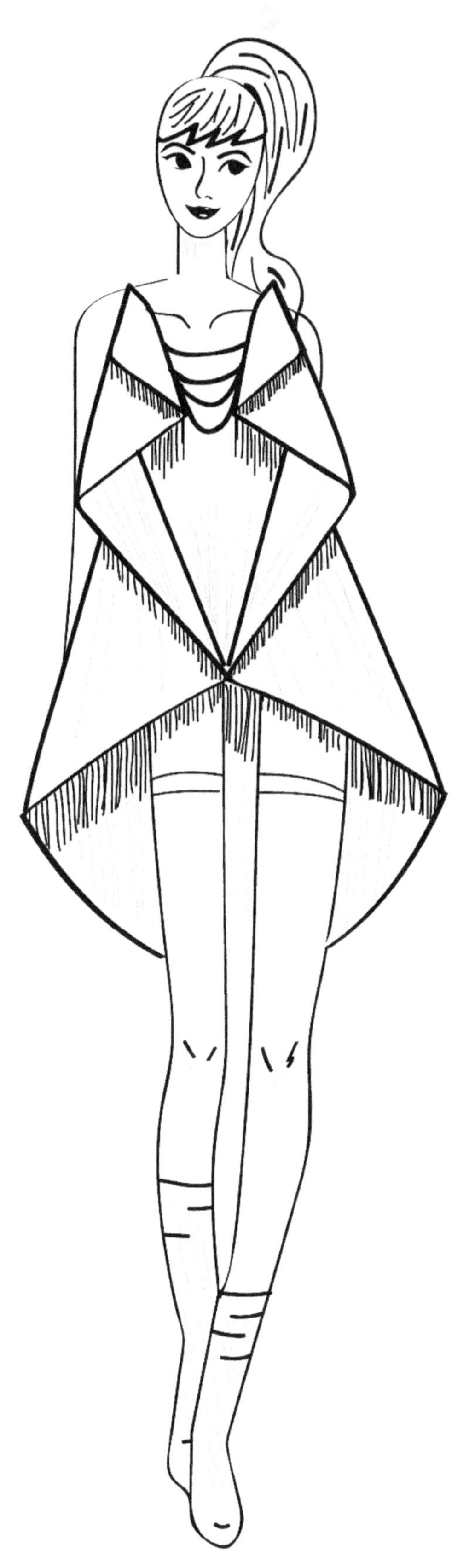

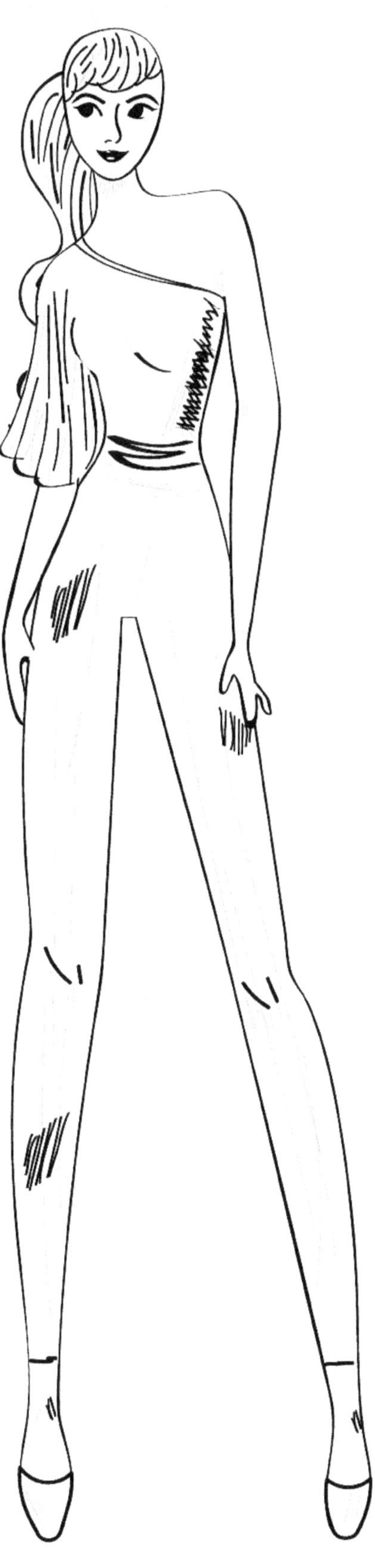

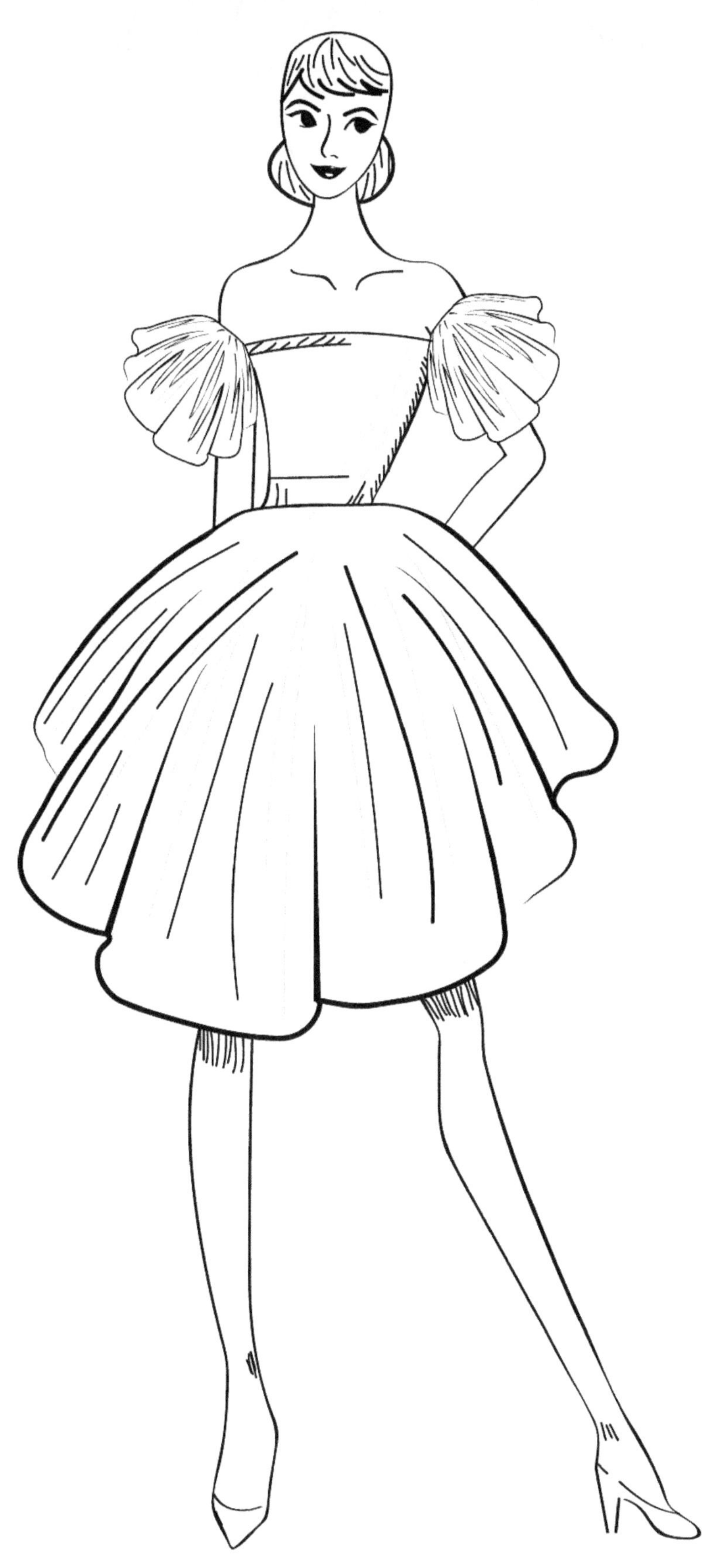

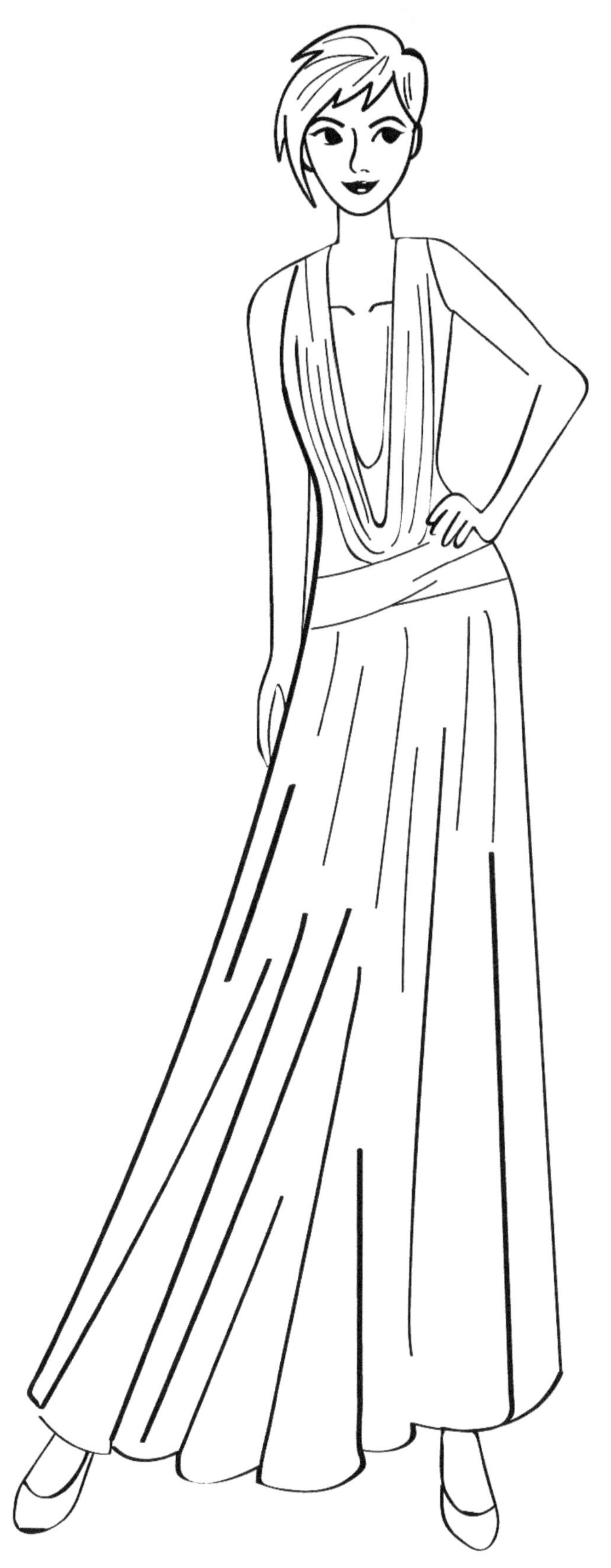

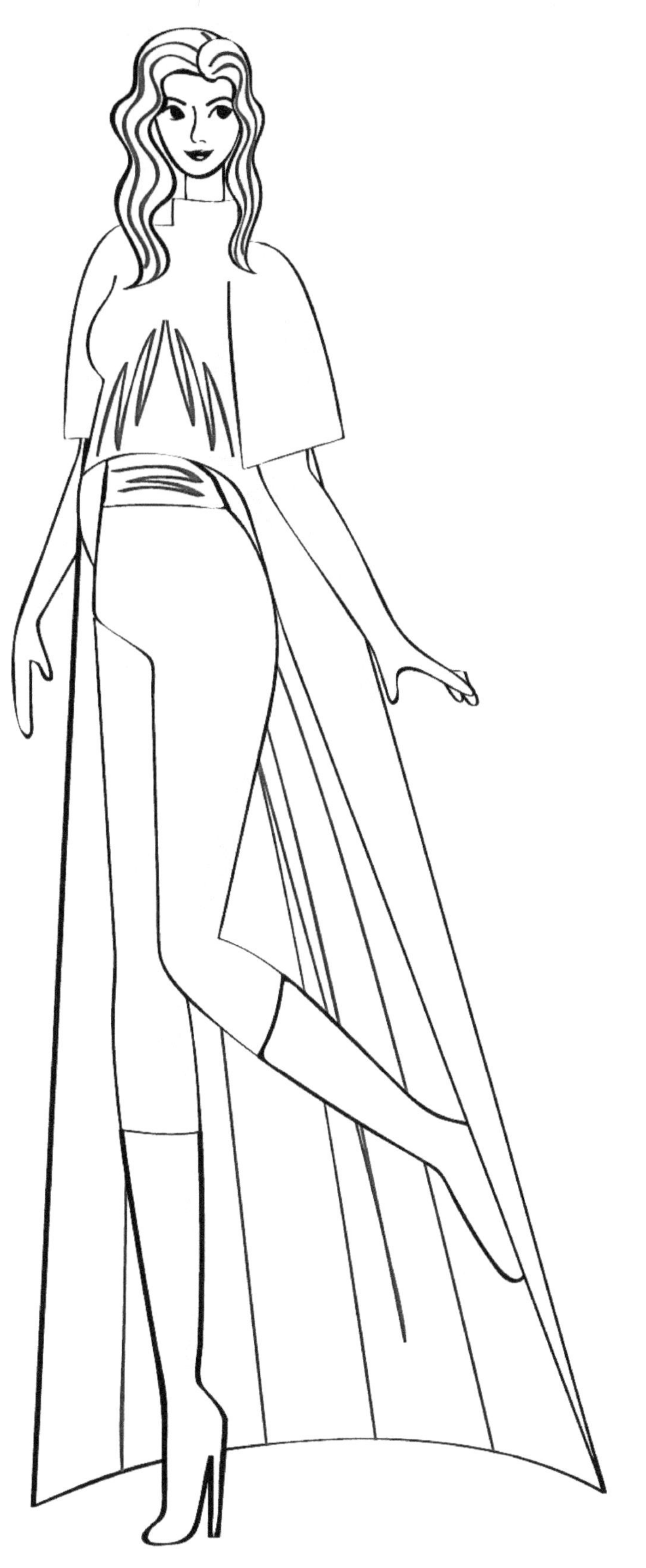

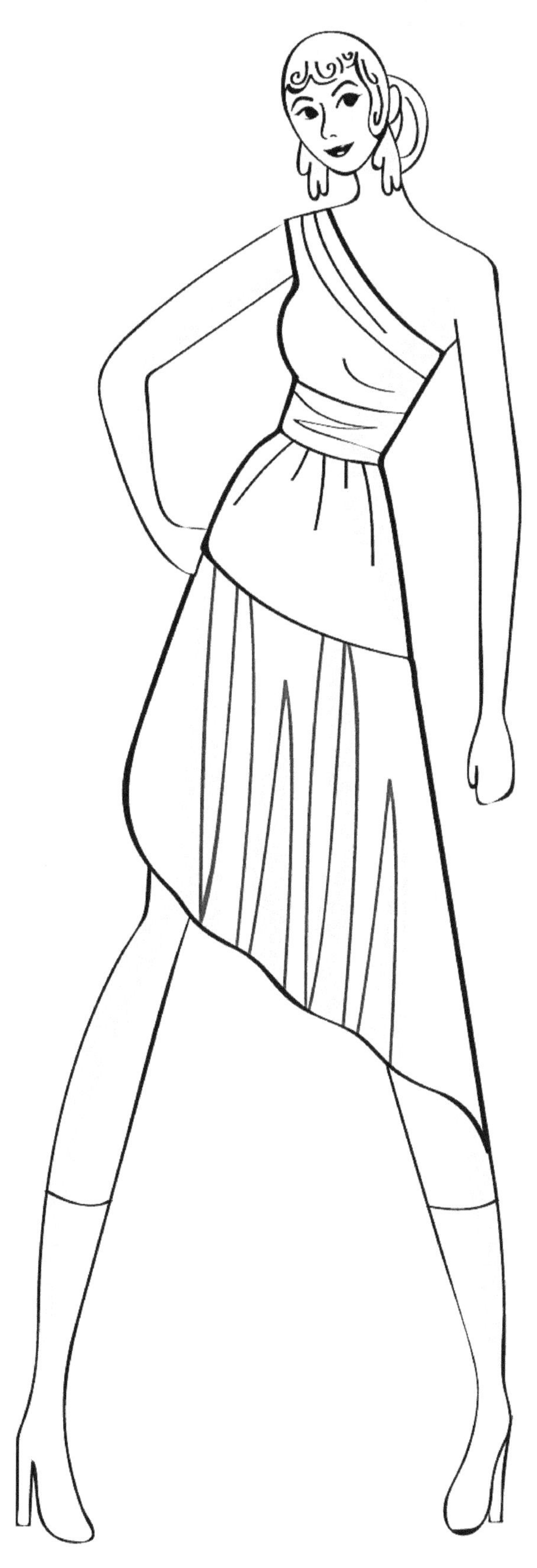

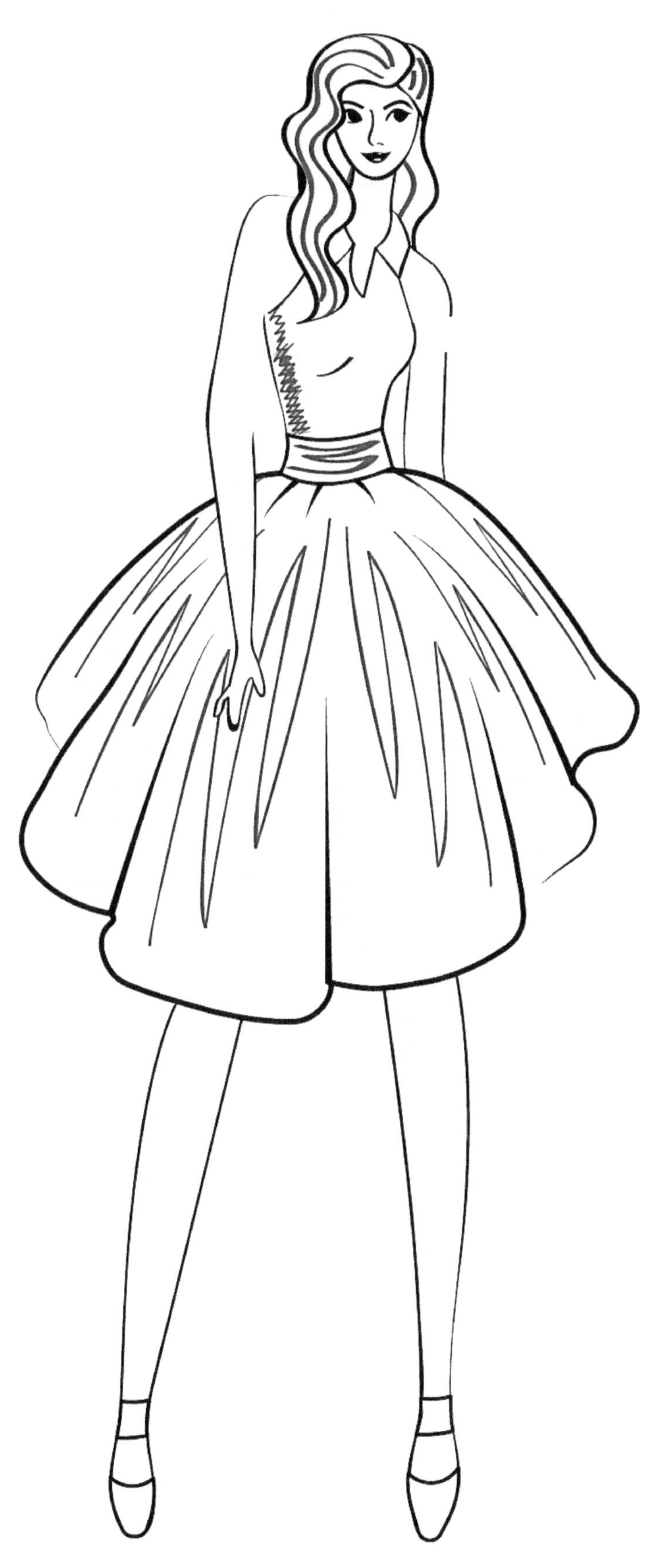

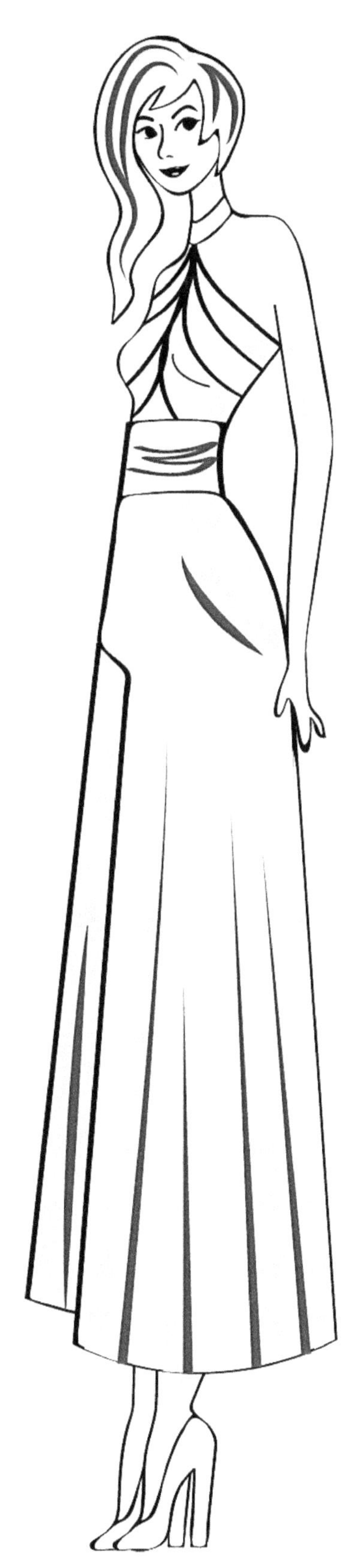

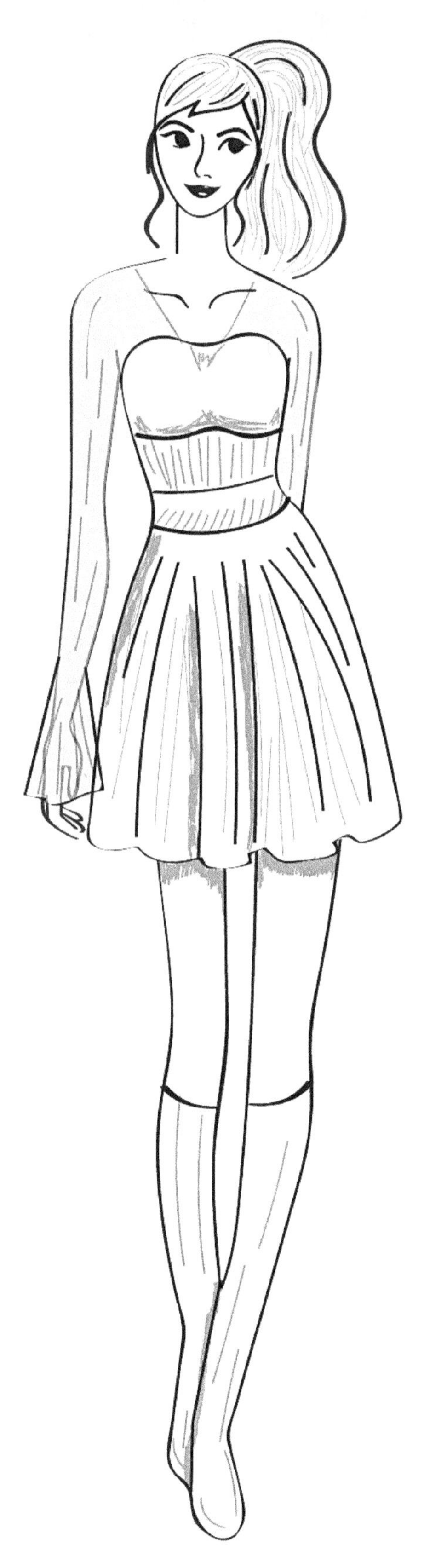

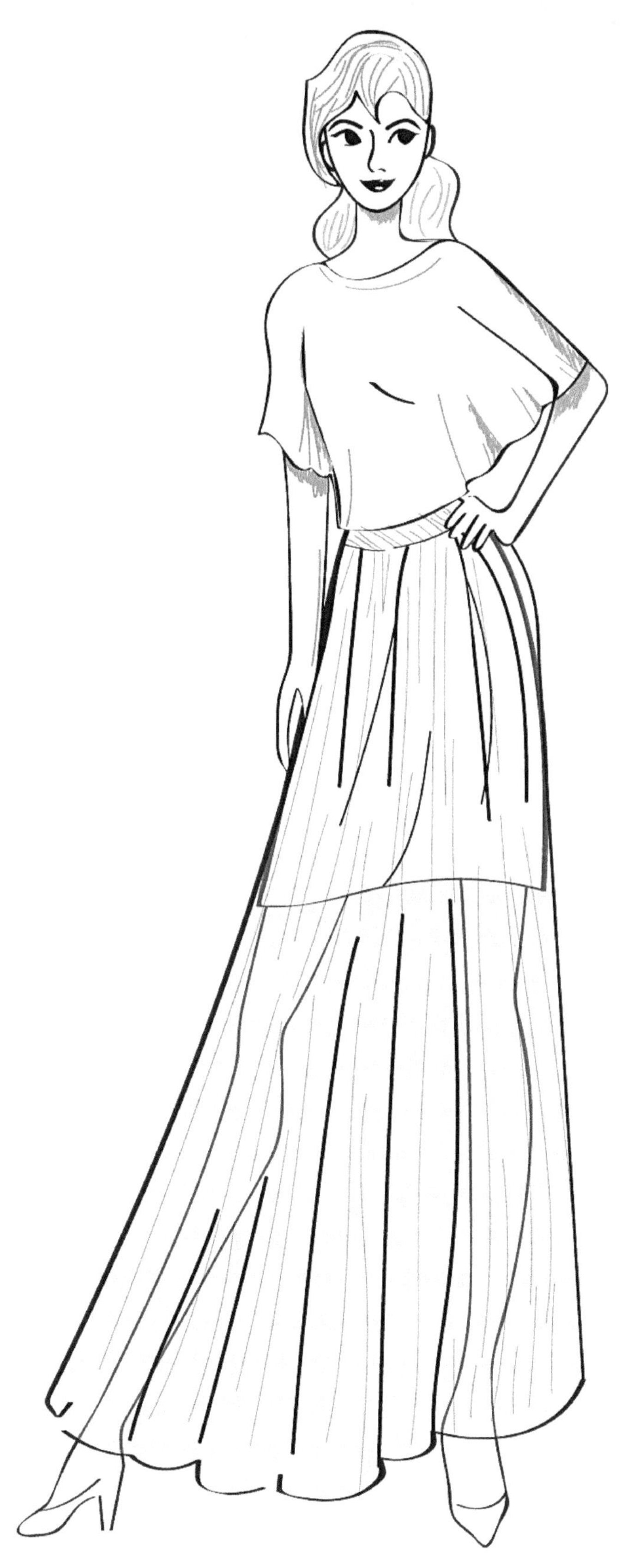

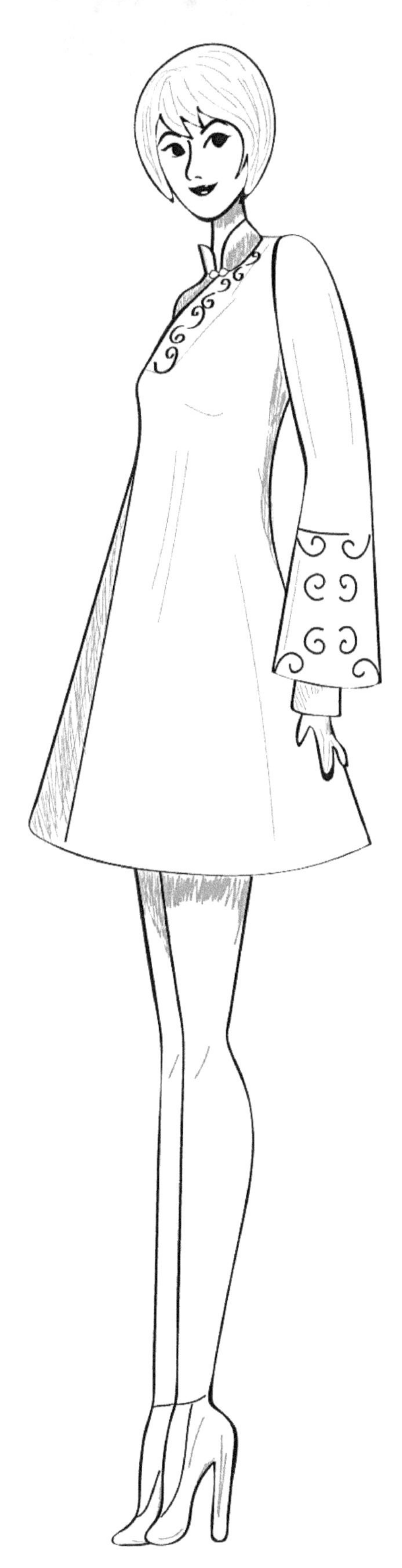

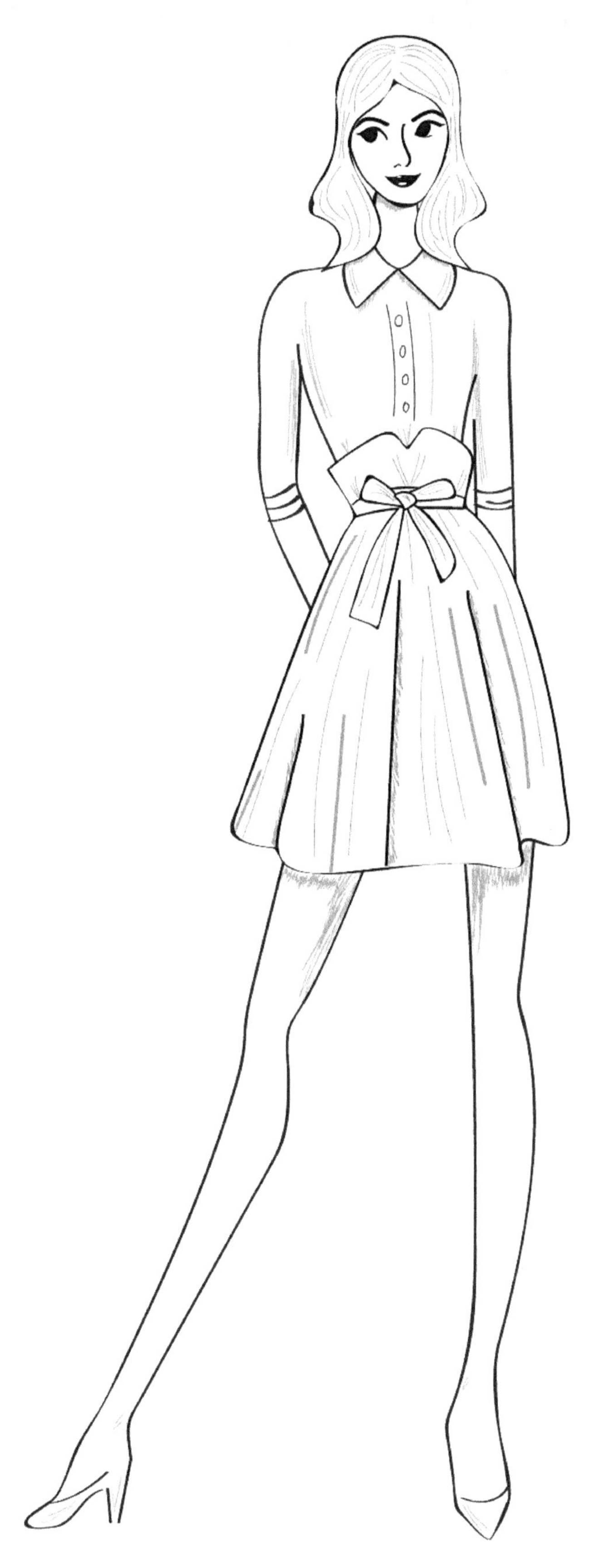

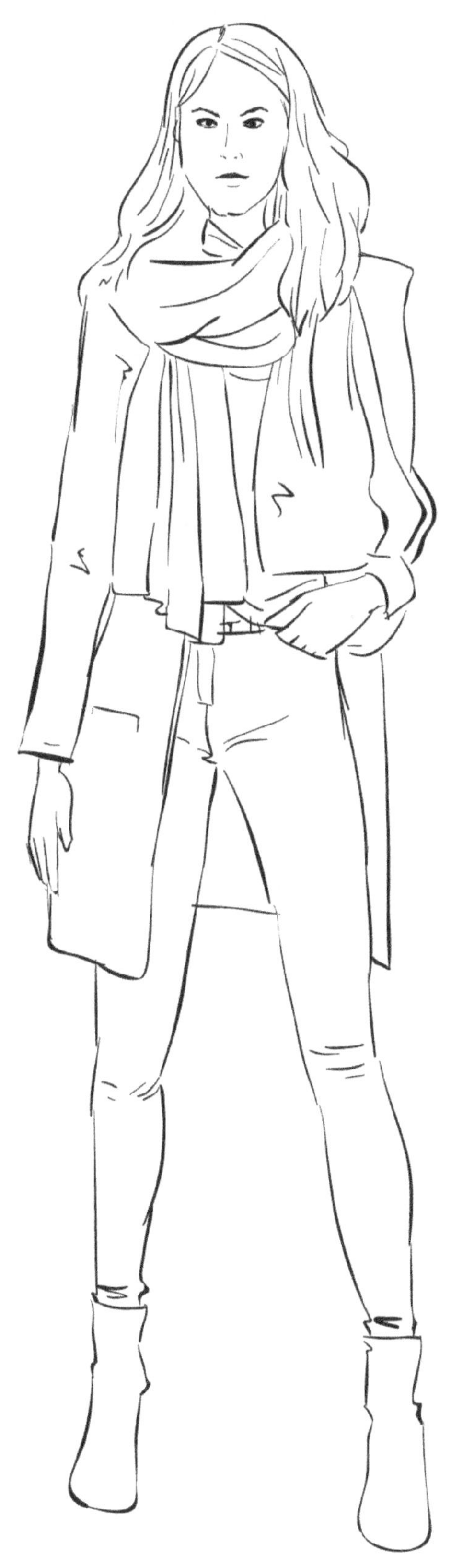

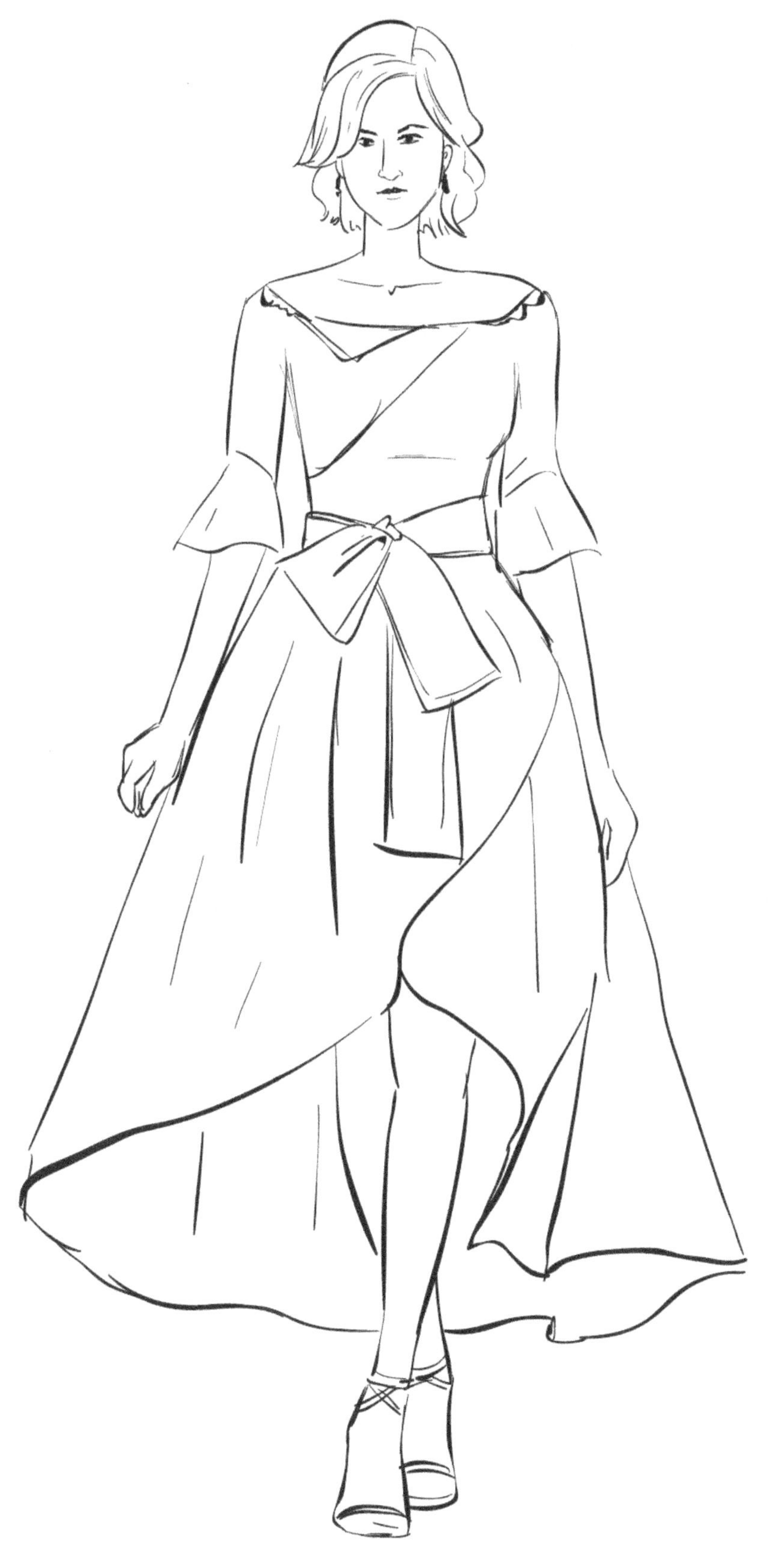

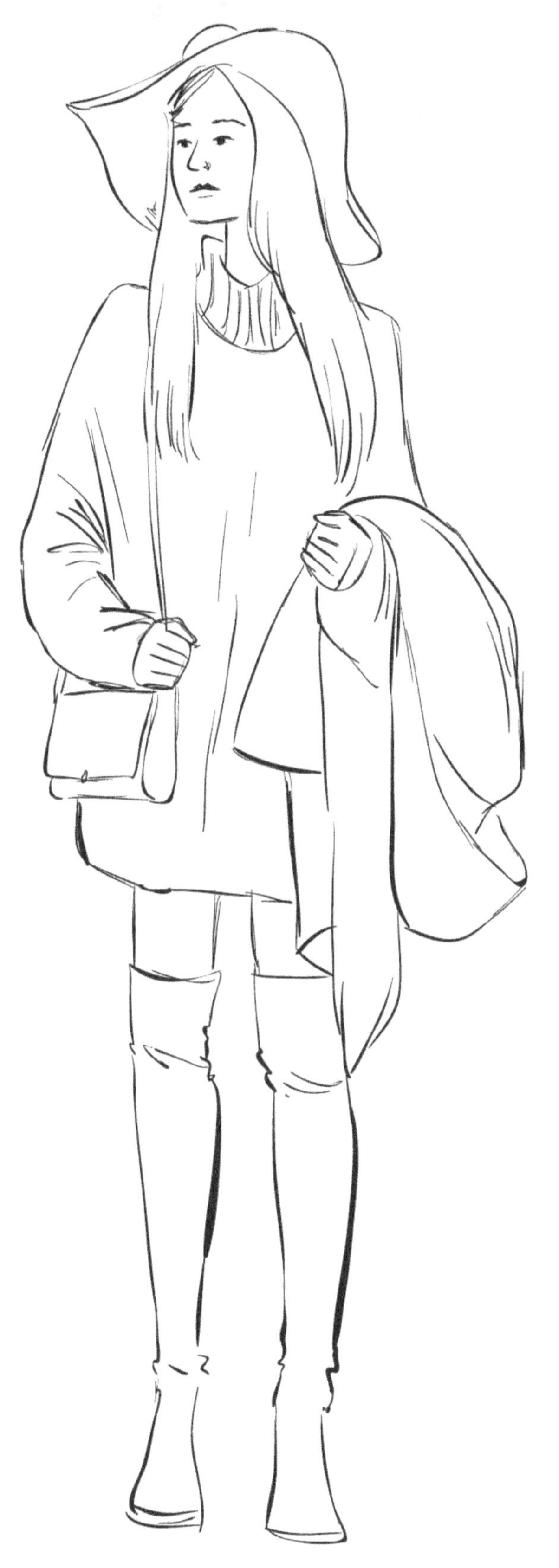

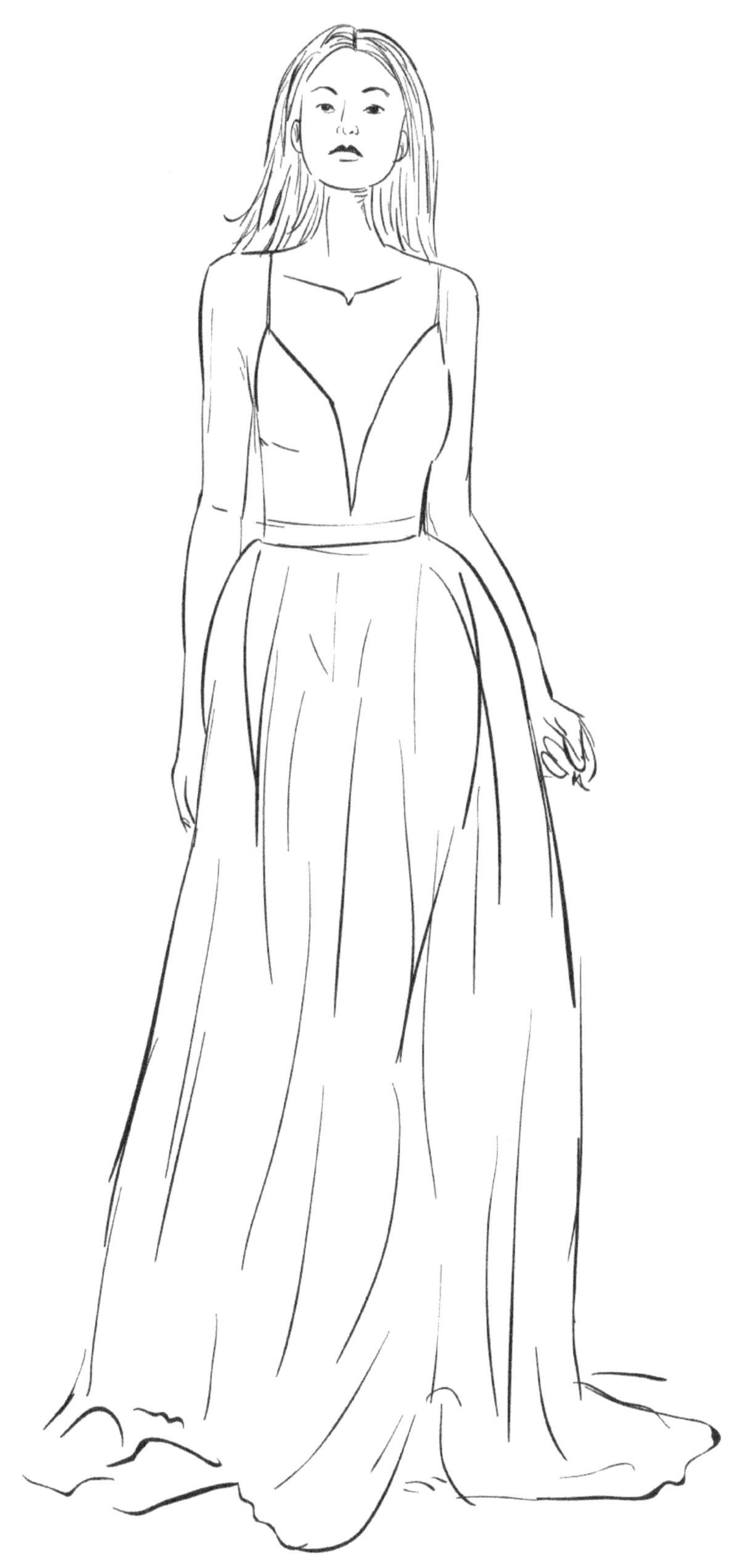

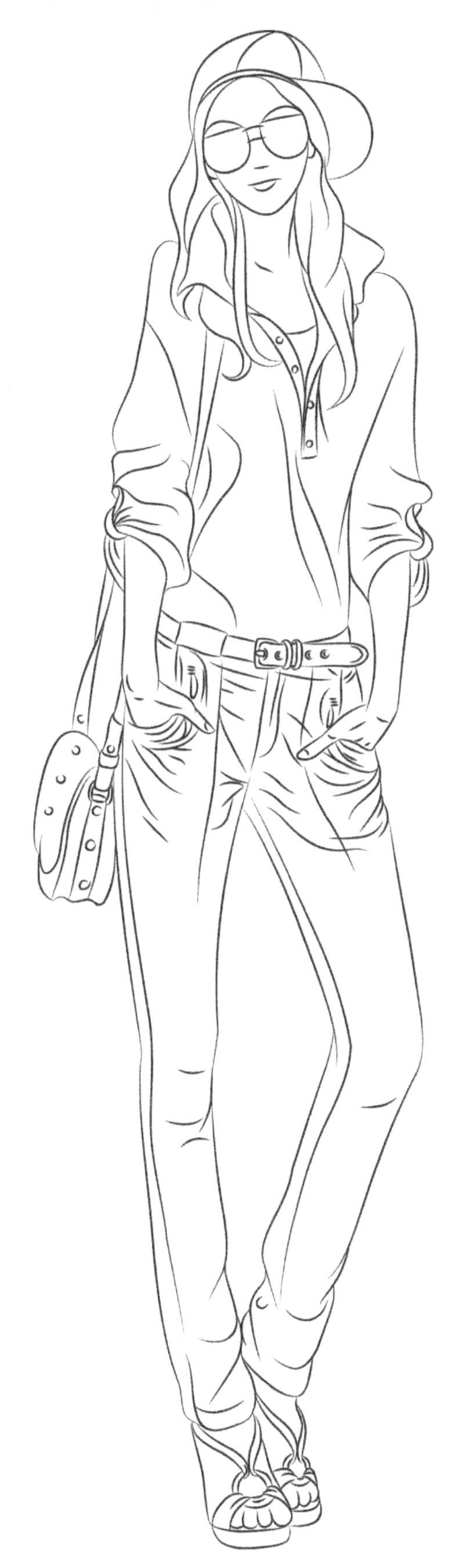

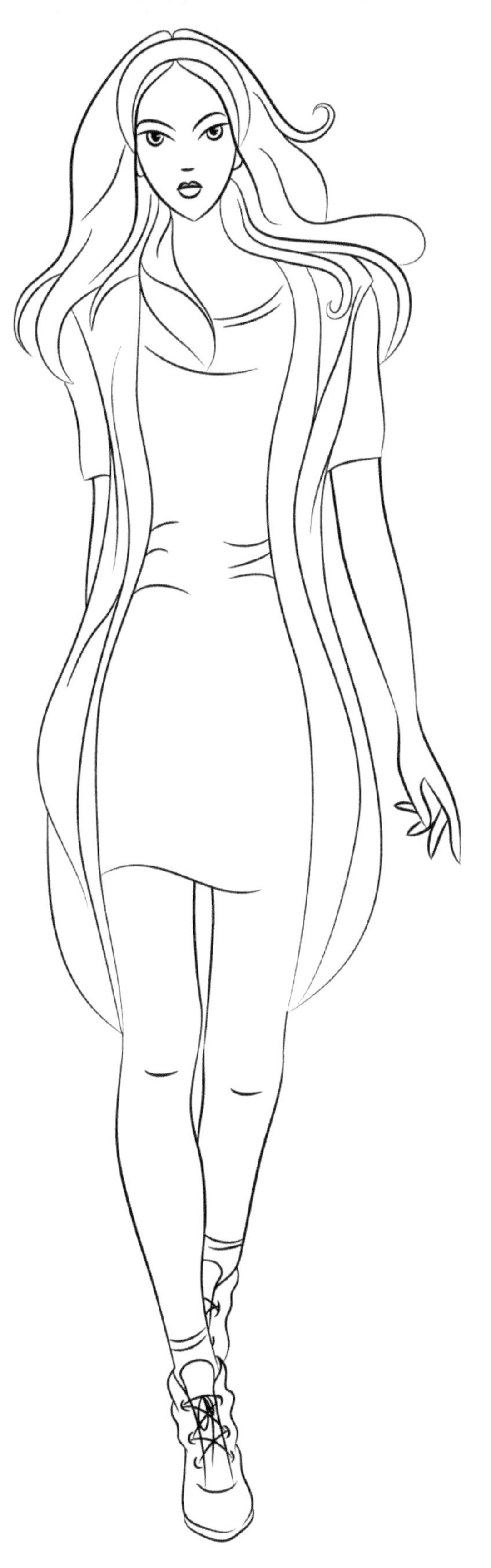

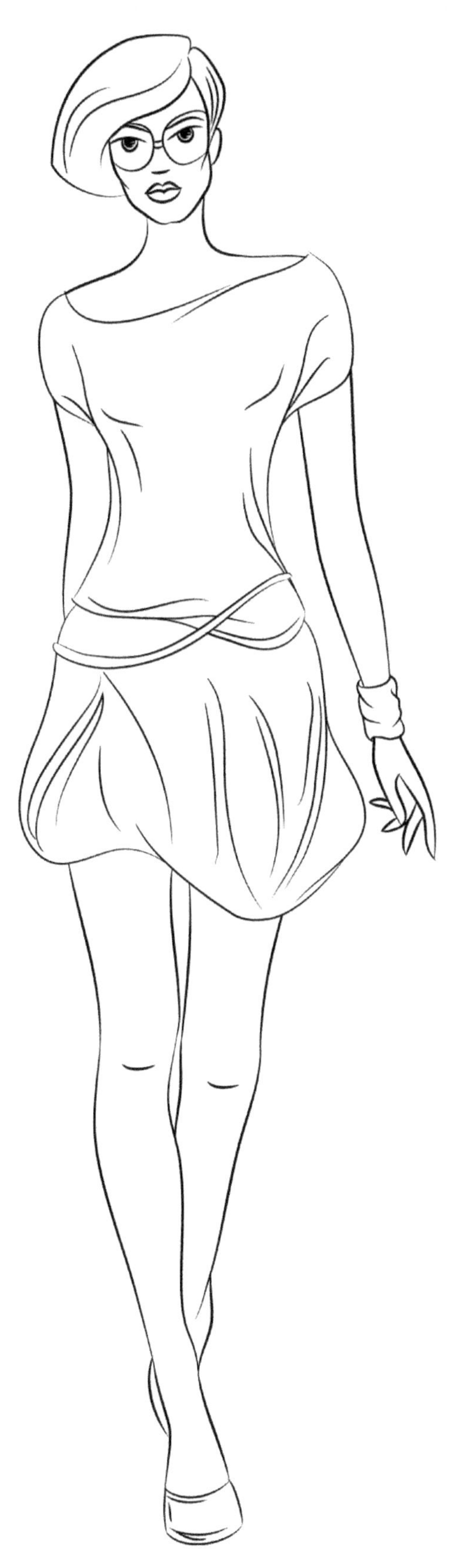

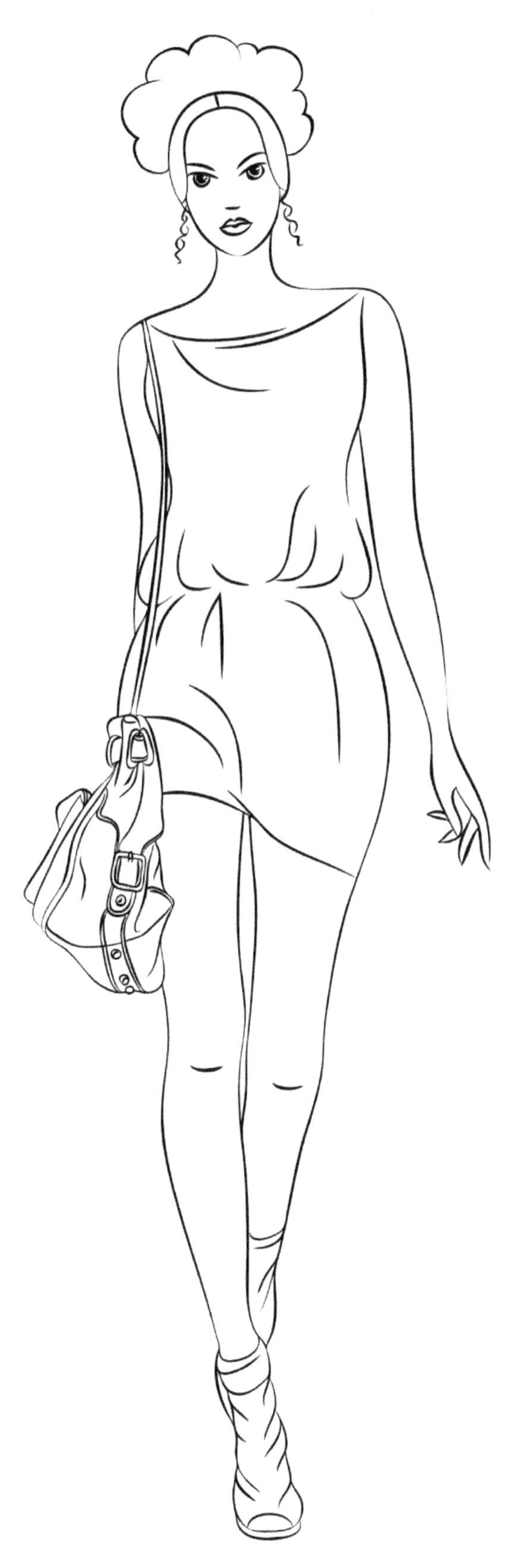

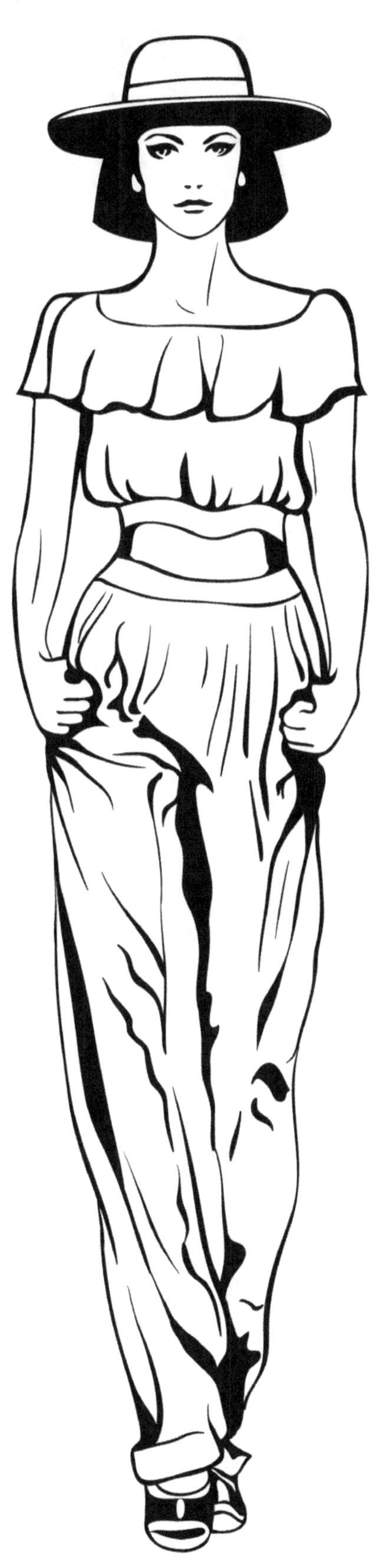

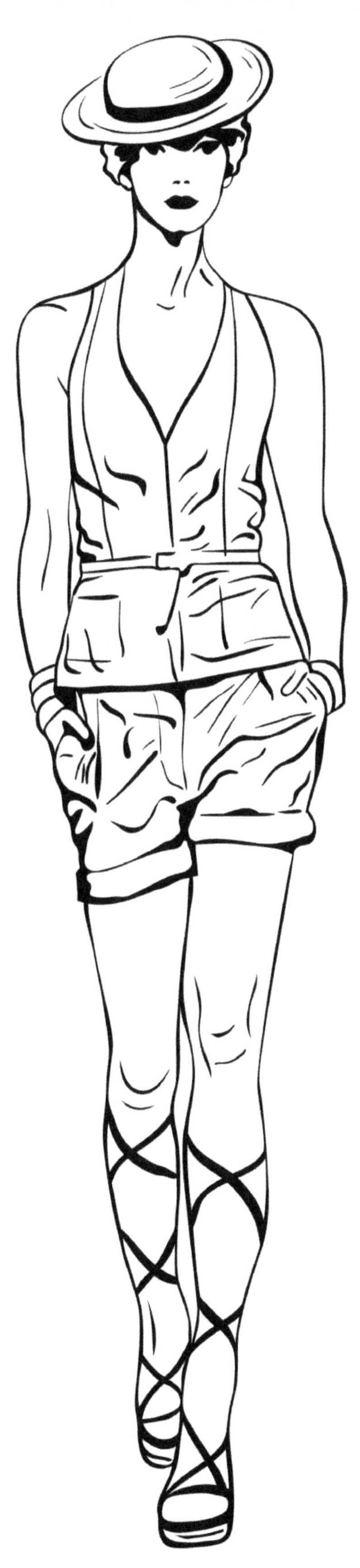

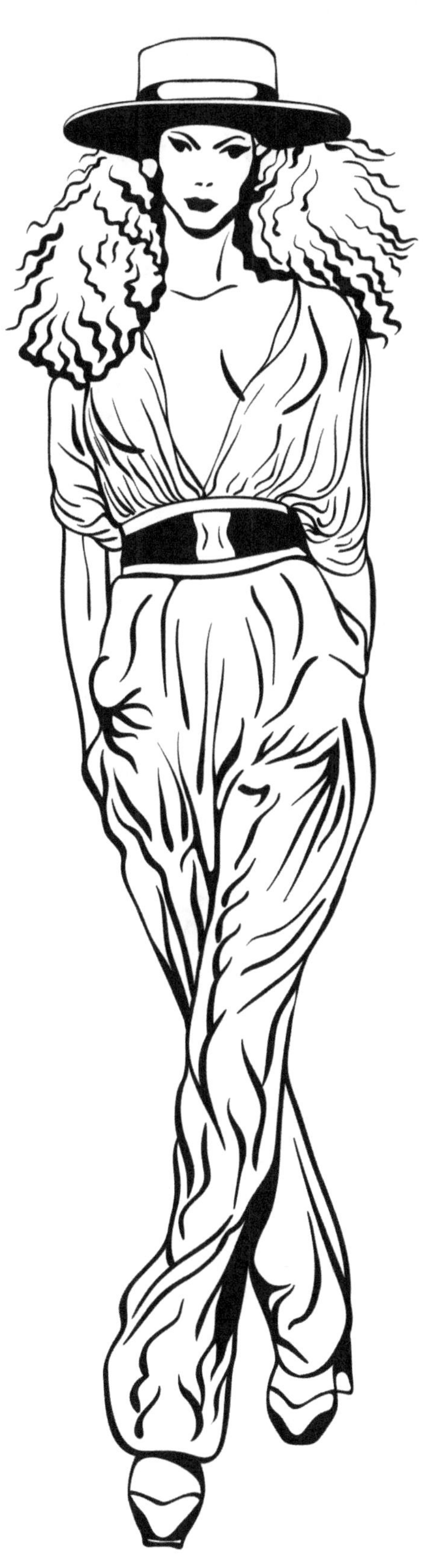

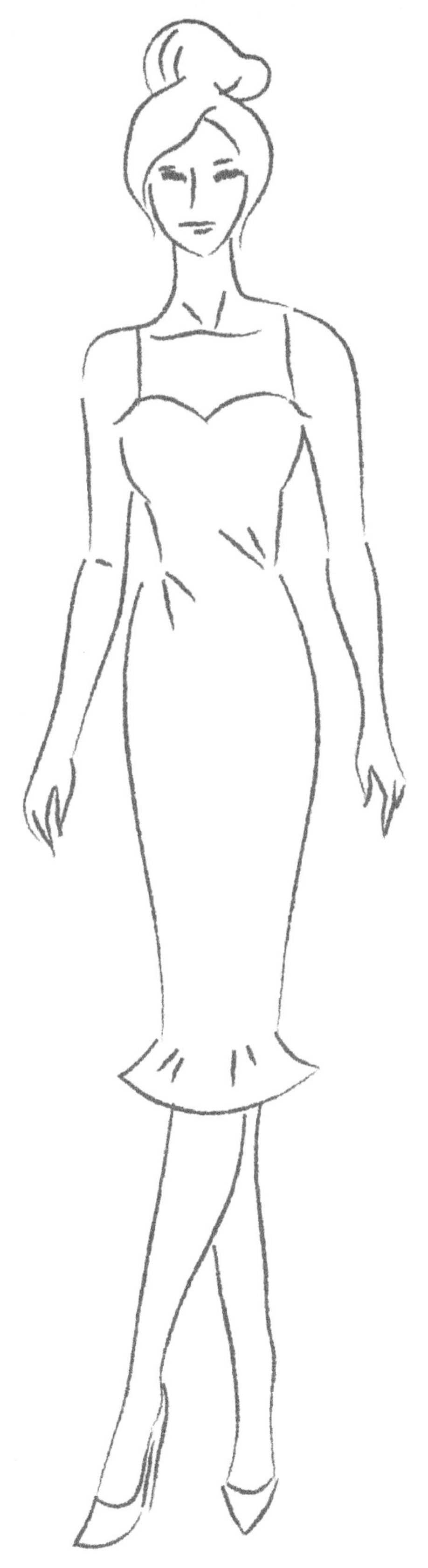

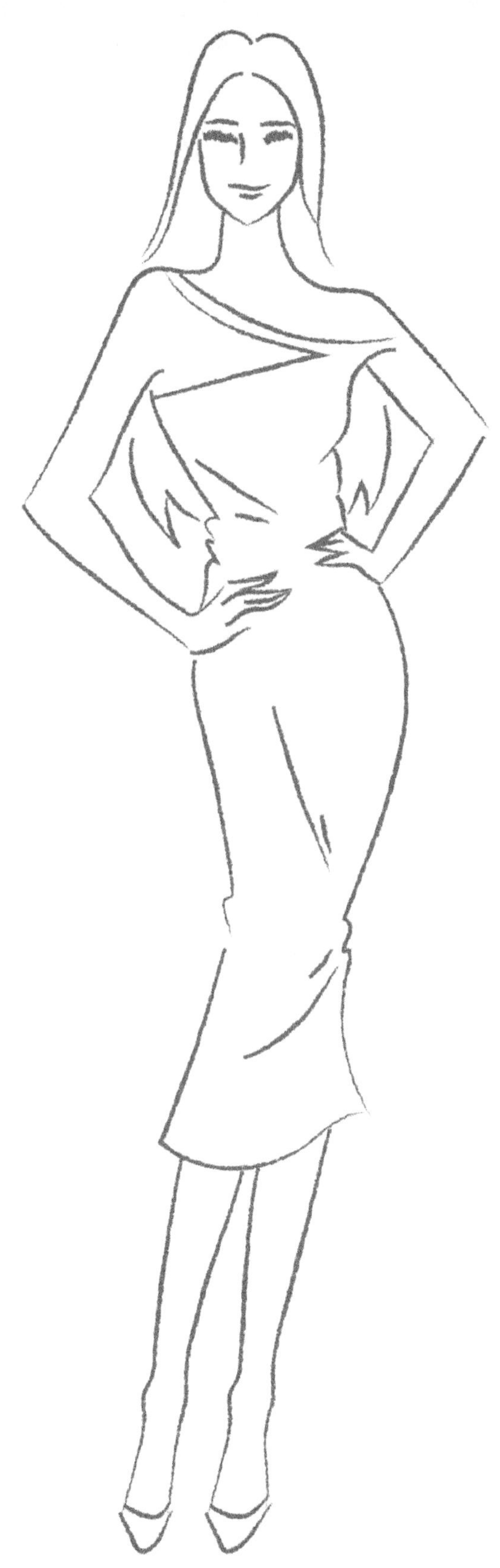

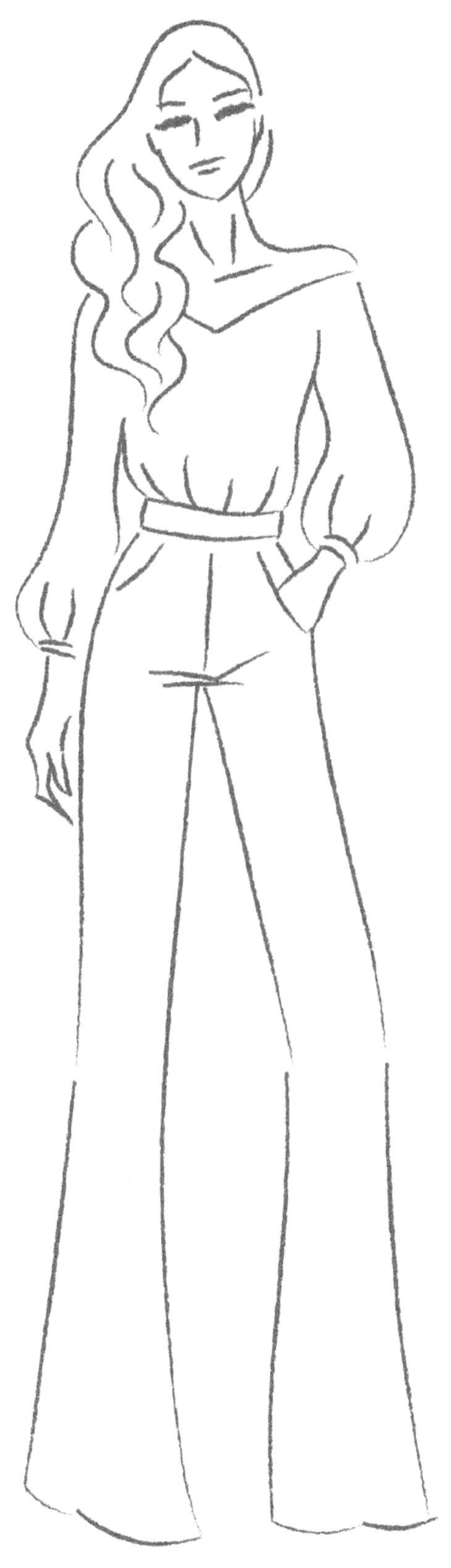

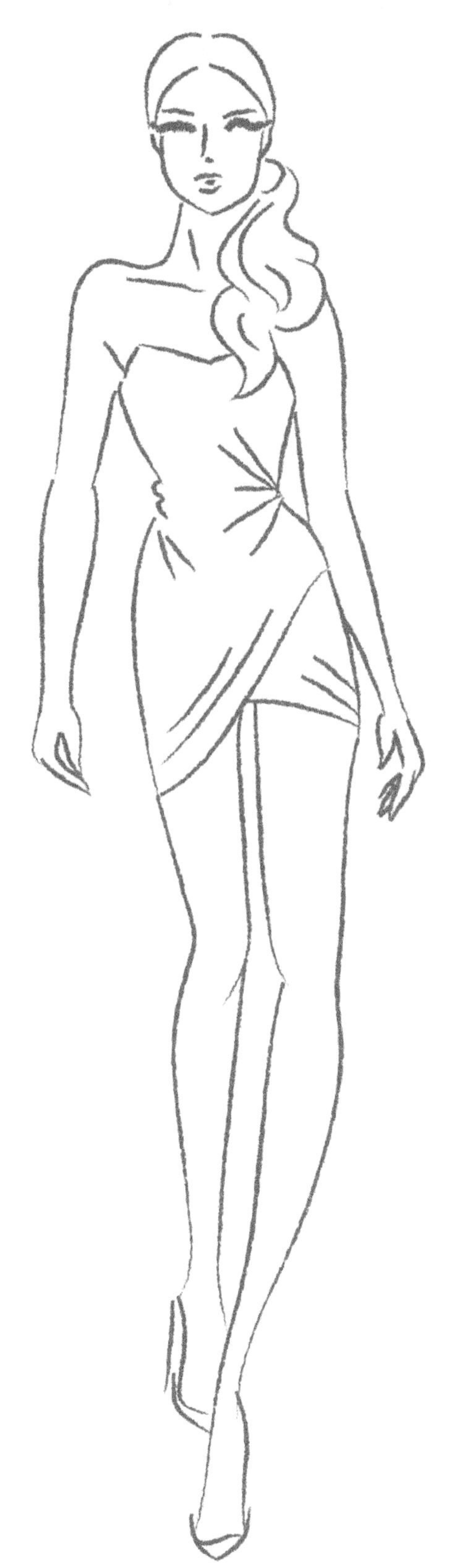

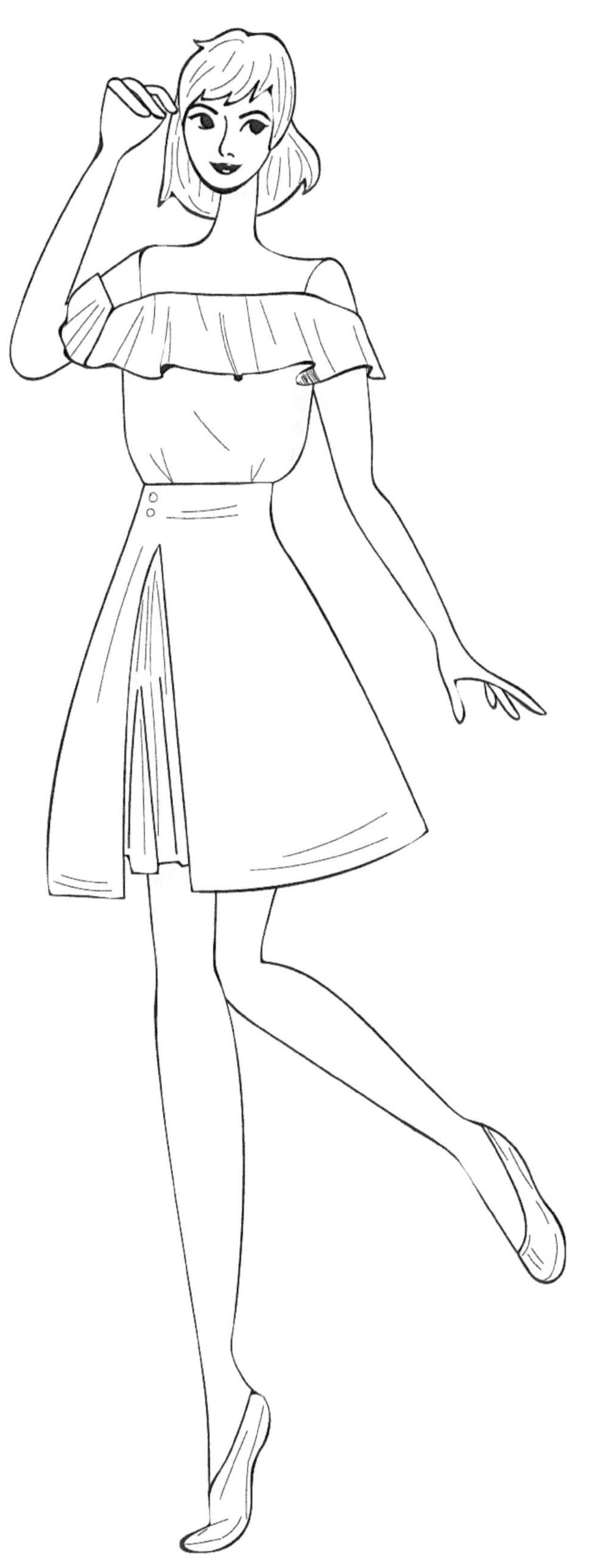

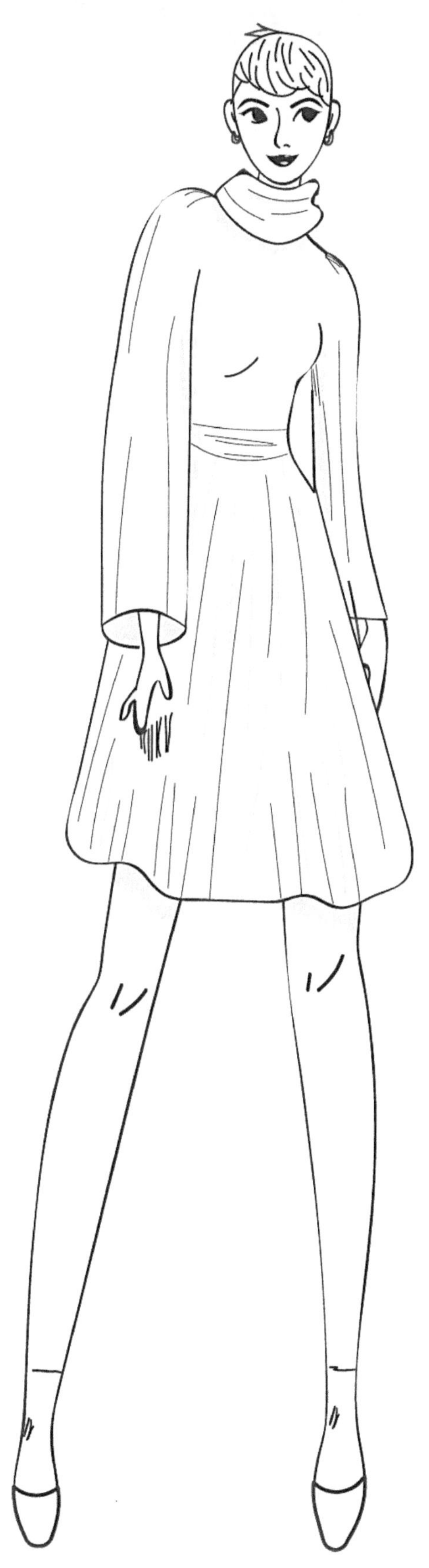

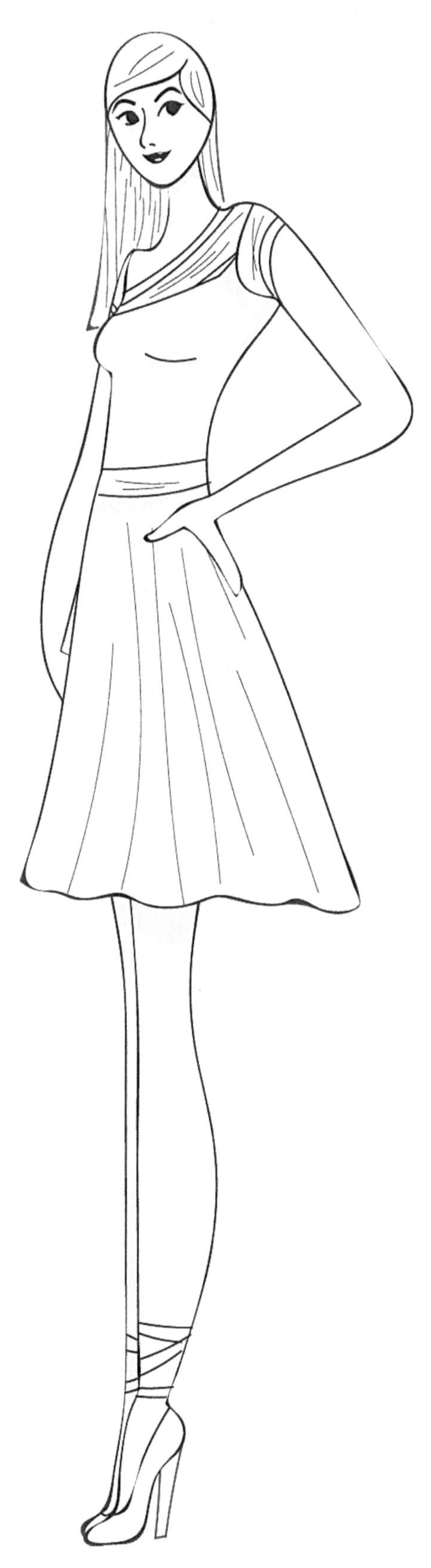

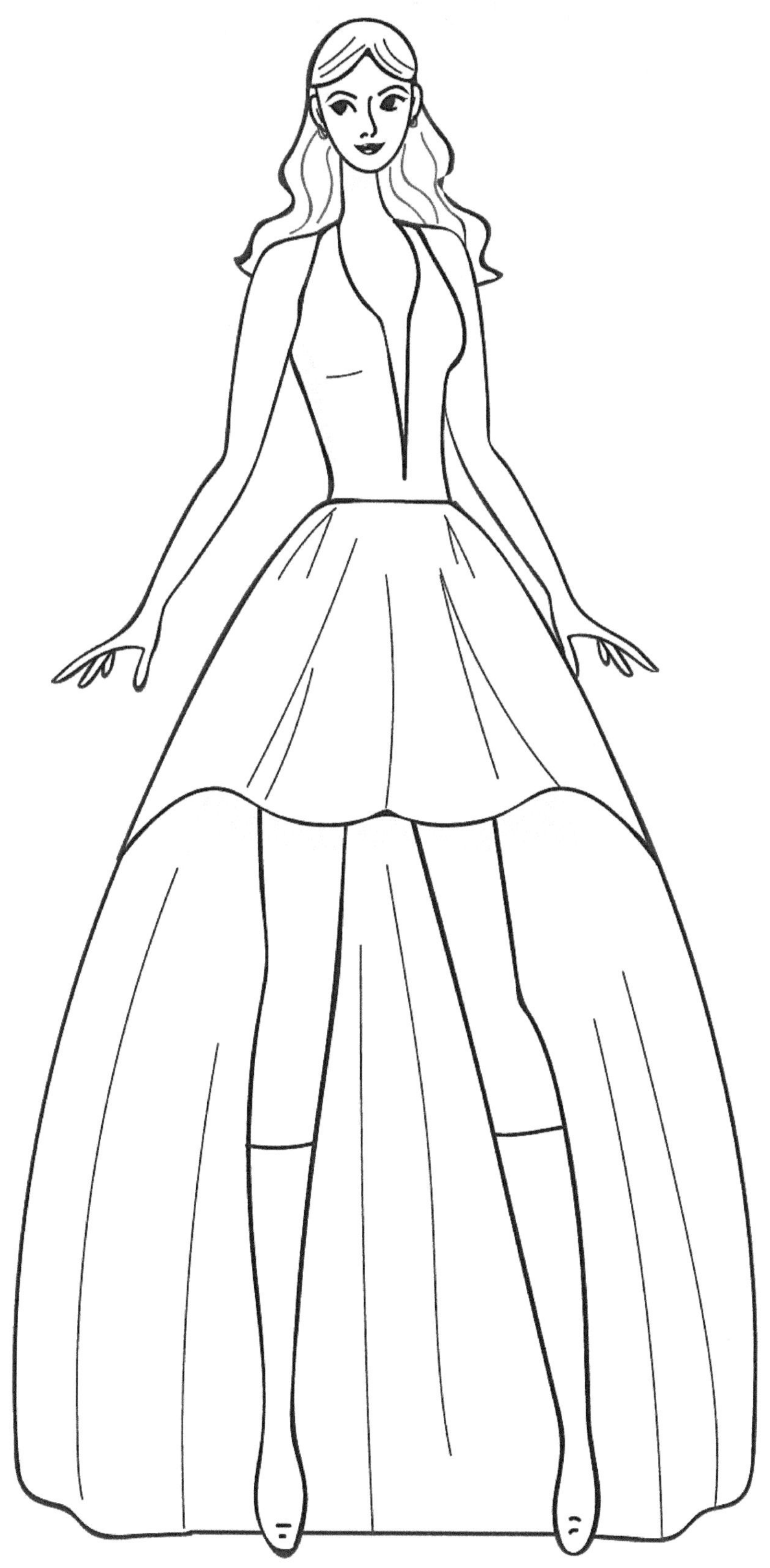

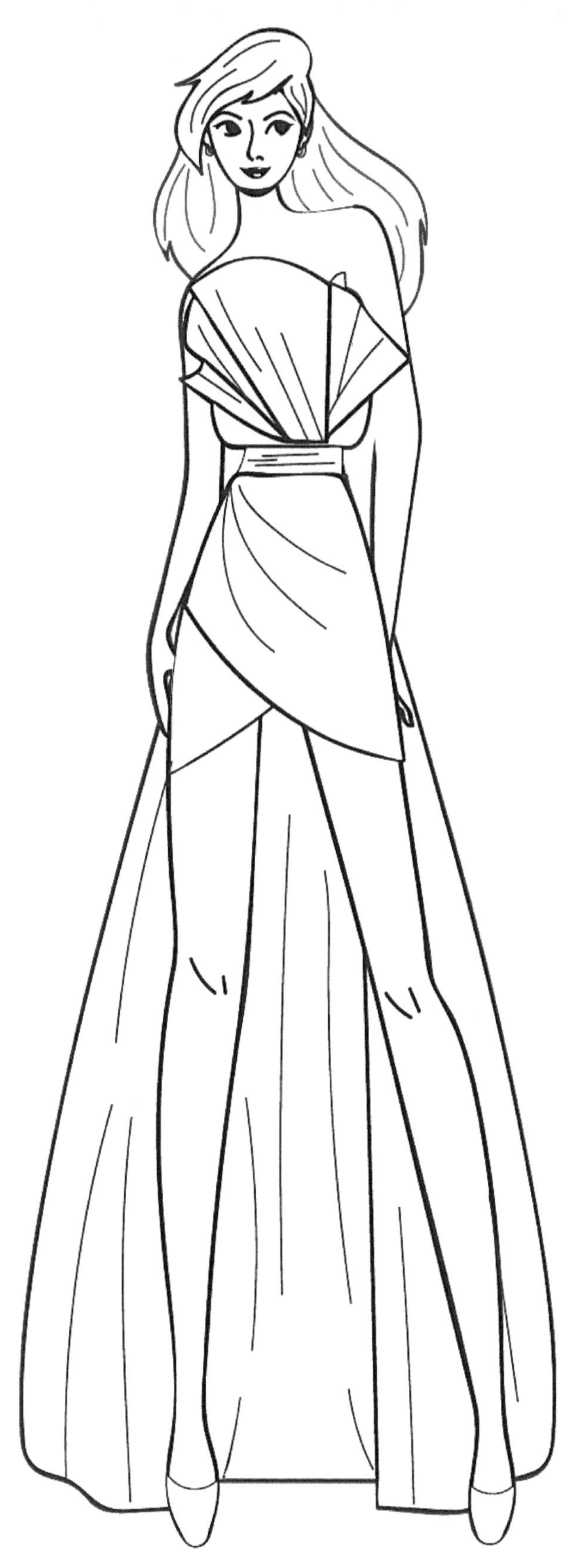

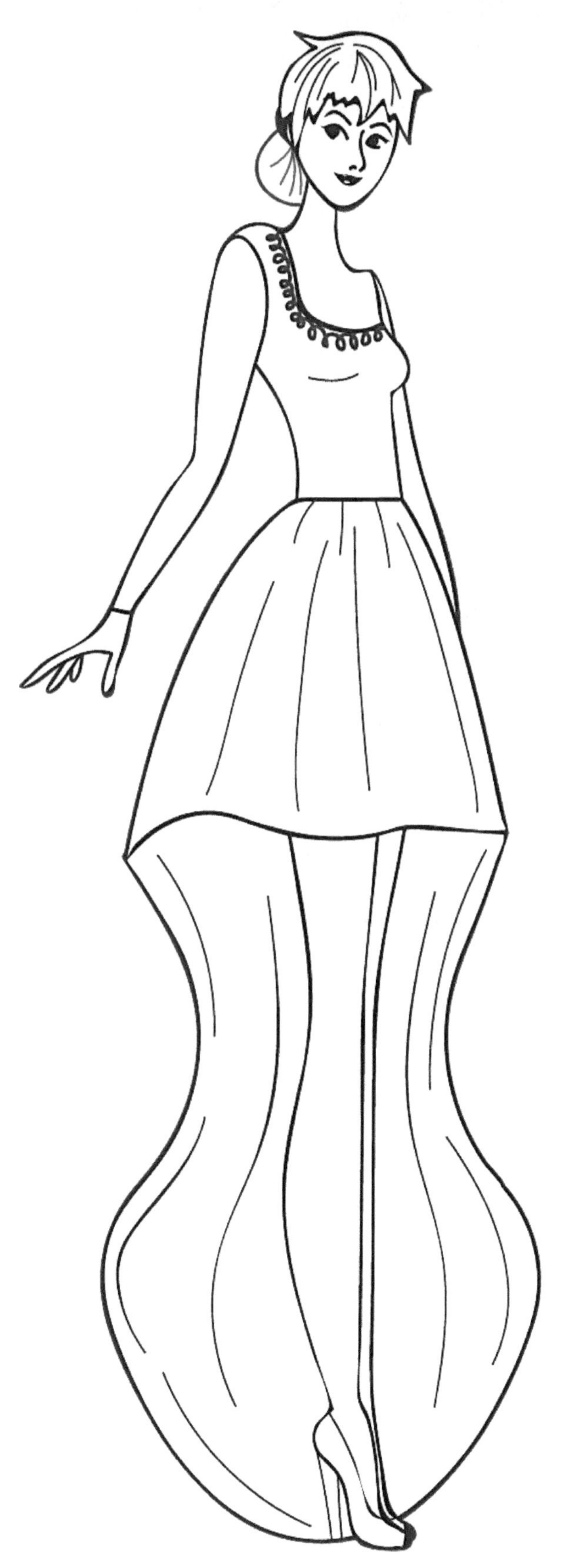

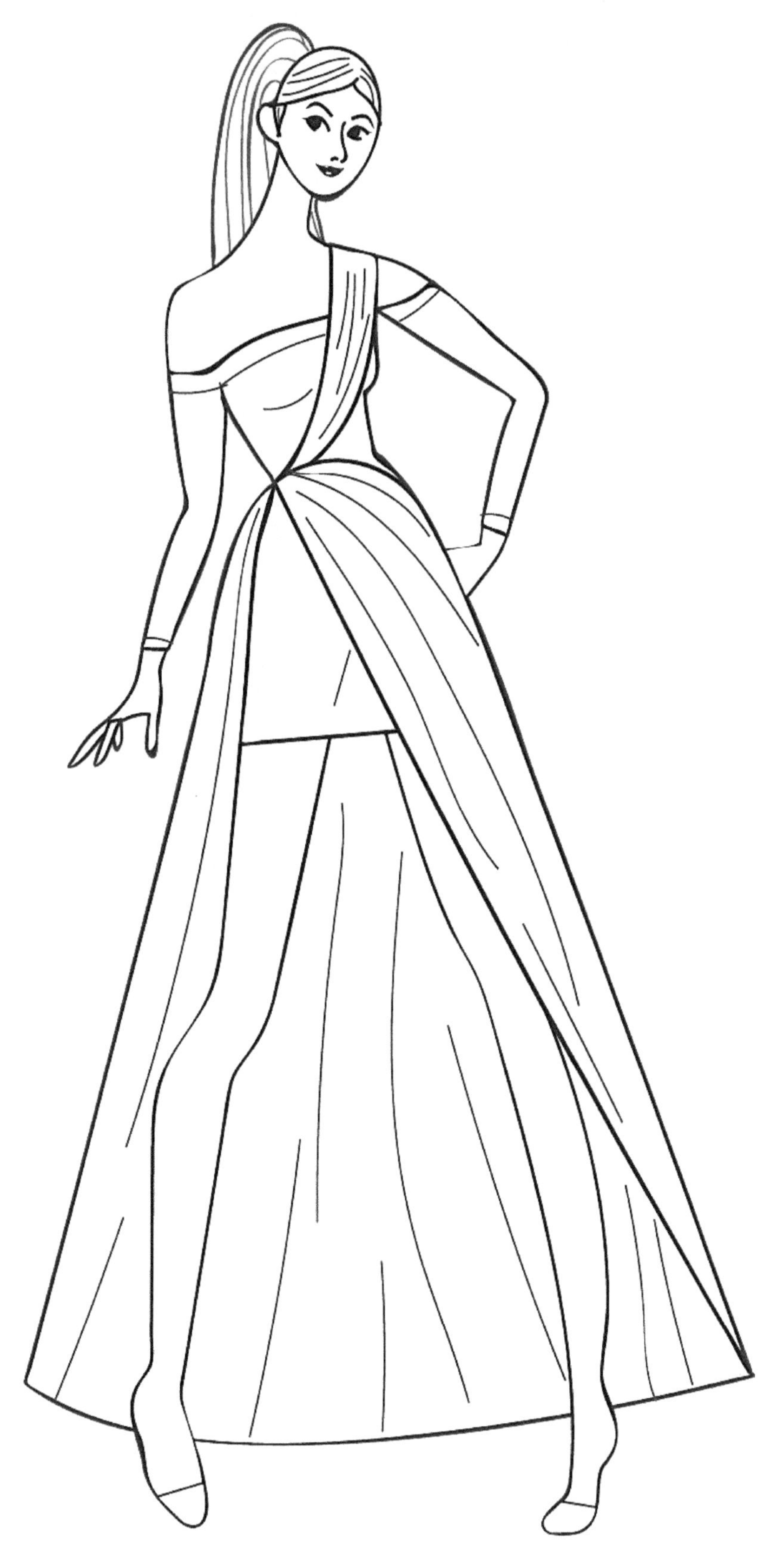

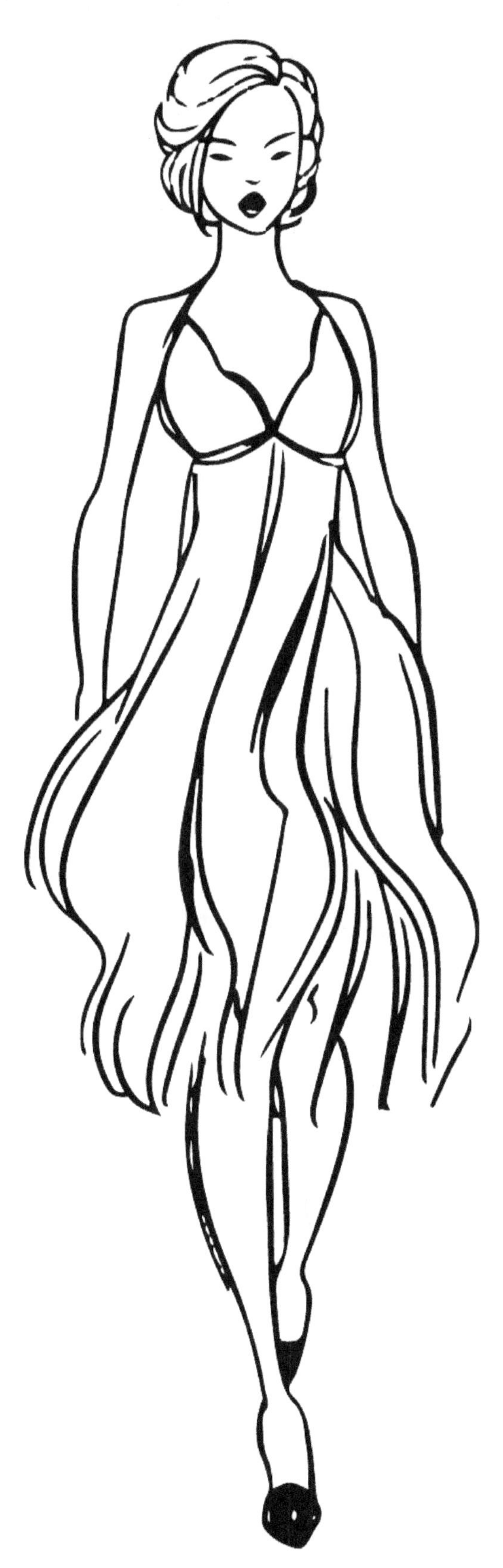

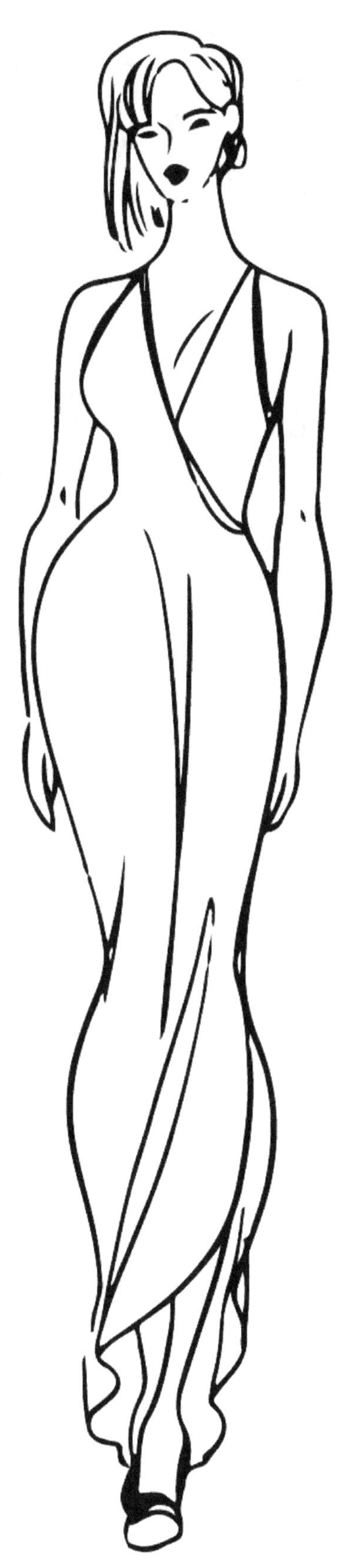

40 Outfits To Style

We hope you enjoyed our
book
As a small family company,
your feedback is very
important to us.
Please let us know
how you like our
book at :
drcipcom@gmail.com

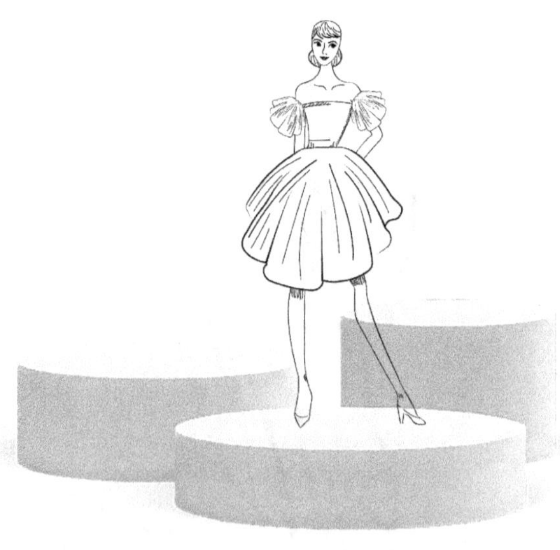